i

This is for all the amazing parents and guardians – Your dedication to protecting, teaching, and supporting your children is truly inspiring. May this book be a helpful guide on your journey.

Table of Contents

Introduction 2

Why Digital Parenting Matters.. 4

Understanding the Online World Your Child Navigates................... 5

How Children Use the Internet... 5

Popular Platforms and Their Risks.................................... 7

Common Cyber Threats and Risks.. 7

How to Use This Book: A Step-by-Step Guide.............................. 9

Part 1: Understanding the Online World.................................. 11

Chapter 1: The Digital Landscape for Kids 12

The Rise of the Internet and Social Media 12

How Kids and Teens Use Technology Today 13

Common Ways Kids Use Technology:................................14

Common Online Platforms and Their Risks (Social Media, Gaming, Messaging Apps)..15

The Psychological Impact of Digital Exposure on Children 18

Chapter 2: Cyber Threats Every Parent Should Know 22

Cyberbullying: What It Is and How It Happens 22

Understanding Cyberbullying...22

How Cyberbullying Happens...24

Signs Your Child Might Be a Victim.................................24

How Parents Can Help 24

Online Predators: How They Target Kids 25

Who Are Online Predators? 25

Where Do They Operate? 25

How They Lure Kids 26

How to Protect Your Child 27

Privacy Risks: The Dangers of Oversharing 27

Why Oversharing is Dangerous 27

What Shouldn't Be Shared? 27

Steps to Reduce Privacy Risks 27

Inappropriate Content: Exposure to Violence, Hate Speech, and
Adult Content 28

Where Kids Encounter Harmful Content 28

How to Keep Kids Safe 29

Scams and Phishing Attacks on Kids 29

What Are Scams and Phishing Attacks? 29

Common Scams Targeting Kids 29

How Kids Can Avoid Scams 30

Final Thoughts 30

Part 2: Monitoring & Supervising Your Child's Digital Life 32

Chapter 3: Setting Digital Boundaries for Kids 33

Understanding Age-Appropriate Internet Use 33

Why Age-Appropriate Internet Use Matters 33

Guidelines for Different Age Groups 34

Creating a Family Digital Agreement 36

Why a Digital Agreement is Important.............................36

Steps to Creating a Family Digital Agreement...................37

Establishing Screen Time Limits That Work 38

How to Set Effective Screen Time Limits.......................39

Encouraging a Healthy Online-Offline Balance..................39

Strategies to Maintain a Digital-Real Life Balance 40

Chapter 4: Parental Controls & Monitoring Tools.............41

Setting Up Parental Controls on Devices and Apps.............41

Understanding Parental Controls..............................41

How to Set Up Parental Controls on Common Devices............41

YouTube's Safety Features....................................44

Turn on Restricted Mode:.....................................44

Use YouTube Kids: 44

Google SafeSearch and Family Link...........................45

iOS and Android Safety Settings 45

Monitoring Apps: The Pros and Cons 46

Why Use a Monitoring App?....................................46

Popular Monitoring Apps 46

Tracking Online Activity Without Violating Trust............47

How to Monitor Without Spying................................47

Signs That Monitoring is Needed..............................47

Balancing Safety and Trust 47

Chapter 5: Safe Social Media and Messaging Practices 49

Popular Social Media Platforms (Instagram, Snapchat, TikTok, Discord) 49

Setting Privacy Settings and Restrictions 51

Steps to Set Privacy Settings on Social Media 51

Teaching Kids to Recognize Fake Accounts and Scams.......... 52

How to Identify a Fake Account.. 53

How to Spot and Prevent Cyberbullying............................... 53

Signs That Your Child Might Be Experiencing Cyberbullying... 54

Steps to Prevent and Address Cyberbullying 54

Final Thoughts.. 56

Part 3: Educating and Empowering Your Child............................. 57

Chapter 6: Teaching Kids About Online Safety............................. 58

The Right Way to Talk About Internet Dangers 58

Start With Open Conversations 59

Use Everyday Examples... 59

Encourage Questions and Make It a Two-Way Conversation ... 59

Teaching Kids to Identify and Handle Cyberbullying 60

Helping Kids Recognize Cyberbullying 61

Steps to Handle Cyberbullying... 61

How to Talk About Online Predators Without Scaring Them........ 62

Teach the Concept of Online Strangers............................. 62

What to Do if Someone Seems Suspicious 62

Encouraging Critical Thinking About Online Content............. 63

Teach Them to Spot Fake News and Clickbait 63

Discuss the Influence of Social Media 63

Conclusion: Empowering Kids to Be Smart Digital Citizens 64

Chapter 7: Digital Footprint & Online Reputation 65

What Is a Digital Footprint? 65

How Kids' Online Actions Affect Their Future 66

The Risks of Posting Personal Information 67

How Can Parents Help? 68

Teaching Kids to Think Before They Share 69

Conclusion 70

Chapter 8: Safe Online Gaming for Kids 71

The Risks of Online Gaming (Chat Rooms, Micro transactions, Addiction) 71

Setting Boundaries for Safe Gaming 73

Recognizing and Avoiding In-Game Scams and Predators 74

Selecting Age-Appropriate Games 75

Conclusion 76

Part 4: Protecting Your Child from Cyber Threats 77

Chapter 9: Cybersecurity Basics for Families 78

Creating Strong Passwords and Using Two-Factor Authentication 78

The Importance of Strong Passwords 78

Two-Factor Authentication (2FA): Adding an Extra Layer of Security 80

How to Enable Two-Factor Authentication 81

Safe Browsing Practices for Kids 82

Why Safe Browsing Matters 82

Tips for Safe Internet Browsing.. 82

Avoiding Scams and Phishing Attacks 84

What Are Scams and Phishing Attacks?............................ 84

How to Spot a Phishing Scam... 84

What to Do If You or Your Child Falls for a Scam............ 84

How to Handle a Hacked Account....................................... 85

Signs That an Account Has Been Hacked 85

Steps to Recover a Hacked Account 85

Final Thoughts... 86

Chapter 10: Dealing with Cyberbullying 87

How to Spot Signs Your Child is Being Cyberbullied....... 87

Steps to Take if Your Child is a Victim............................. 89

Teaching Kids to Respond to Online Harassment 90

When to Report Cyberbullying (to Schools, Platforms, Law Enforcement) 91

Final Thoughts... 92

Chapter 11: Protecting Kids from Online Predators.............. 93

How Predators Lure Kids Online 93

Warning Signs to Watch for in Your Child's Online Behavior........ 95

Steps to Take If You Suspect Online Grooming 97

Final Thoughts... 99

Part 5: Advanced Strategies for Digital Parenting 100

Chapter 12: Raising Tech-Savvy and Responsible Digital Citizens **101**

Teaching Kids Ethical Online Behavior 101

Understanding Digital Ethics 102

Steps to Teach Ethical Online Behavior 103

Helping Kids Navigate Misinformation and Fake News 103

Understanding Fake News and Misinformation 104

Steps to Teach Kids Critical Thinking About Online Content. 104

Encouraging Responsible Technology Use in Schools 105

Why Responsible Tech Use Matters in Schools 105

Strategies to Promote Responsible Technology Use in Schools 106

Conclusion 107

Chapter 13: Preparing for the Future of Technology **108**

The Rise of AI, Virtual Reality, and the Metaverse 108

Understanding Artificial Intelligence (AI) 108

How AI Affects Children's Digital Lives: 108

Exploring Virtual Reality (VR) 109

Potential Benefits of VR for Kids: 109

Understanding the Metaverse 110

Key Features of the Metaverse: 110

How Emerging Tech Will Change Kids' Online Experience.......... 110

The Shift from Passive to Immersive Experiences 111

The Expansion of AI-Powered Education 111

Greater Risks in Digital Security and Privacy 112

Preparing Kids for Future Digital Trends 112

Conclusion 114

Conclusion **116**

The Role of Parents in Shaping Digital Behavior 116

Leading by Example 117

Staying Actively Involved 117

Final Digital Parenting Checklist 118

Encouraging Open Communication About Online Safety 120

Building Trust Through Honest Conversations 120

Creating a Safe Space for Sharing 120

Keeping Communication Ongoing 121

Final Thoughts 121

Additional Resources **123**

Parental Control Apps Comparison Chart 123

Why Parental Control Apps Are Essential 123

Parental Control Apps Comparison Chart 124

Choosing the Right Parental Control App 125

List of Safe Websites & Apps for Kids 125

Why It's Important to Guide Kids Toward Safe Online Spaces
....125

Safe Websites & Apps for Kids 126

Encouraging Safe Online Exploration 126

Final Thoughts 127

Introduction

Parenting has always been a challenging journey, but the rise of technology and the internet has added a whole new layer of complexity. In today's world, children are growing up surrounded by digital devices, online platforms, and social media networks. Unlike previous generations, where screen time was limited to television, today's children have constant access to the internet through smartphones, tablets, laptops, and even smartwatches. This digital transformation brings incredible opportunities for learning, entertainment, and social interaction. However, it also introduces a wide range of risks and challenges that parents must navigate.

Many parents feel overwhelmed by the speed at which technology evolves. New apps, online trends, and digital platforms emerge almost daily, making it difficult to keep up. Additionally, children tend to embrace these technologies quickly, often outpacing their parents in digital literacy. This can create a knowledge gap, leaving parents unsure of how to guide their children toward responsible and safe online behavior.

The challenge of digital parenting is not just about limiting screen time or preventing online addiction. It involves equipping children with the skills to protect themselves from online predators, avoid cyberbullying, recognize misinformation, and practice responsible digital citizenship. More than ever, parents need to be proactive in educating themselves about the digital world to provide their children with a safe and supportive online experience.

Why Digital Parenting Matters

The internet is an integral part of modern life. Children use it for education, entertainment, communication, and even socialization. While the digital world offers countless benefits, it also comes with significant dangers. Without proper guidance, children can be exposed to cyberbullying, online predators, privacy breaches, and inappropriate content. Digital parenting is about ensuring that children develop healthy and responsible online habits while minimizing these risks.

Many parents assume that simply monitoring their child's online activity is enough to keep them safe. However, digital parenting goes beyond supervision. It requires open communication, teaching critical thinking skills, and setting clear boundaries. Parents who actively engage with their children's digital lives can help them make smarter decisions, recognize threats, and use technology responsibly.

In addition, digital parenting fosters trust between parents and children. Instead of making technology a source of conflict, it can become an opportunity for meaningful discussions and shared experiences. When children feel supported rather than controlled, they are more likely to seek parental guidance when facing online challenges.

With cyber threats constantly evolving, parents must stay informed and adaptable. By taking an active role in digital parenting, you are not only protecting your child but also preparing them for a future where technology will play an even bigger role in their lives.

Understanding the Online World Your Child Navigates

The internet is a vast and complex environment, filled with both opportunities and risks. To effectively guide your child, it is essential to understand the various aspects of their online experience.

How Children Use the Internet

- **Education:** Online learning has become a fundamental part of modern education. Many schools use digital platforms for assignments, research, and communication.
- **Entertainment:** Streaming videos, online games, and social media provide endless entertainment options for children and teenagers.

- **Communication:** Messaging apps, social media, and gaming platforms allow children to stay connected with friends and family.
- **Creativity and Expression:** Many children express themselves through digital content, such as videos, blogs, and artwork shared online.

While these uses can be beneficial, they also come with potential dangers. Children may unknowingly interact with strangers, share too much personal information, or come across harmful content. Understanding where and how your child spends time online is the first step in ensuring their safety.

Popular Platforms and Their Risks

Children and teens frequently use platforms like YouTube, TikTok, Instagram, Snapchat, and Discord. While these platforms offer socialization and creativity, they also pose risks such as:

- **Cyberbullying:** Hurtful comments, online harassment, and peer pressure can affect children's self-esteem.
- **Privacy Risks:** Many children do not understand the importance of privacy settings and may share personal details publicly.
- **Online Predators:** Some individuals exploit online platforms to build relationships with children for harmful purposes.
- **Addiction and Overuse:** Excessive screen time can interfere with sleep, school performance, and mental health.

By familiarizing yourself with the digital world, you can better guide your child toward safe and responsible online behaviors.

Common Cyber Threats and Risks

Every time a child goes online, they may encounter risks that could compromise their safety, privacy, and well-being. Here are some of the most common cyber threats that parents need to be aware of:

1. Cyberbullying

Cyberbullying occurs when children are harassed, threatened, or humiliated online. Unlike traditional bullying, cyberbullying can happen 24/7, making it difficult for children to escape. Victims may receive hurtful messages, be excluded from online groups, or have personal information shared without consent.

2. Online Predators

Predators use social media, gaming platforms, and chat apps to befriend children, often pretending to be someone their age. They use manipulation to gain trust and may attempt to exploit children in harmful ways.

3. Privacy and Identity Theft

Children often do not understand the consequences of sharing personal information online. Posting details like their full name, school, or home address can make them vulnerable to identity theft or scams.

4. Inappropriate Content

The internet is full of content that is not suitable for children. Without proper filters, they may accidentally come across violent, explicit, or harmful material that can negatively impact their mental well-being.

5. Scams and Phishing Attacks

Children can easily fall for online scams, such as fake giveaways, phishing emails, or links that download harmful viruses onto their devices. Teaching children to recognize suspicious messages can help prevent them from becoming victims.

By being aware of these risks, parents can take steps to protect their children and teach them how to navigate the digital world safely.

How to Use This Book: A Step-by-Step Guide

This book is designed to be a **practical guide** that helps parents navigate the challenges of raising children in a digital world. To get the most out of this book, follow these steps:

Step 1: Start with Understanding

Read through the first few chapters to understand the digital landscape, common threats, and how children interact with the online world.

Step 2: Assess Your Child's Digital Habits

Observe how your child uses the internet. What platforms do they use? How much time do they spend online? Do they understand online safety rules?

Step 3: Set Up Boundaries and Parental Controls

Use the strategies in this book to set screen time limits, enable parental controls, and establish internet safety rules.

Step 4: Educate and Empower Your Child

Teach your child about digital safety, privacy, and responsible internet use. Encourage open conversations about online experiences.

Step 5: Monitor and Adjust

Digital parenting is an ongoing process. Stay informed about new technologies, update your safety measures, and continue having discussions with your child about their online activities.

By following this guide, you will be equipped with the knowledge and tools to raise a digitally responsible and safe child.

Let's begin this journey together!

Part 1: Understanding the Online World

Chapter 1: The Digital Landscape for Kids

The Rise of the Internet and Social Media

The internet has revolutionized the way we live, work, and communicate. It has become a vast digital world where information, entertainment, and social interaction are just a few clicks away. In the early days, the internet was mainly used for research, emails, and basic browsing. However, with the rise of social media platforms, video-sharing sites, and interactive gaming communities, the internet has transformed into a space where people—especially children and teens—spend a significant portion of their daily lives.

Social media has played a crucial role in shaping this digital landscape. Platforms like Facebook, Instagram, TikTok, and Snapchat have turned the internet into a dynamic space for sharing experiences, connecting with friends, and engaging with content. These platforms are designed to be highly interactive, making them attractive to young users who crave social validation, entertainment, and self-expression. However, while social media offers many benefits, it also introduces various risks, including cyberbullying, privacy concerns, and exposure to inappropriate content.

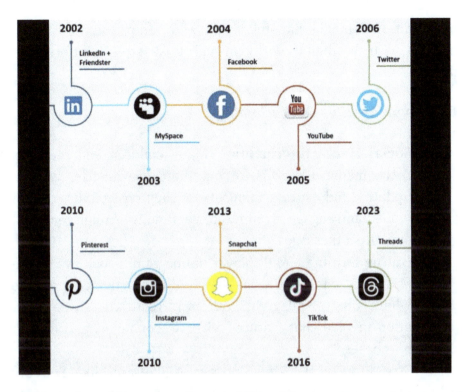

The digital world is expanding rapidly, with new apps, websites, and online communities emerging all the time. This growth has made it essential for parents to understand how children use technology, the platforms they engage with, and the potential risks they might encounter. By gaining this knowledge, parents can take proactive steps to ensure their children have a safe and positive online experience.

How Kids and Teens Use Technology Today

Technology is an integral part of children's lives today. From an early age, kids are exposed to digital devices such as smartphones, tablets, laptops, and gaming consoles. Unlike previous generations that relied

13

on traditional media like television and radio, today's children interact with the digital world through a variety of platforms and devices.

Common Ways Kids Use Technology:

- **Social Media Interaction** – Many children and teens use social media platforms to communicate with friends, share updates, and express themselves. They post pictures, create videos, and engage in online conversations through comments and direct messages.
- **Online Gaming** – Multiplayer online games such as Fortnite, Minecraft, and Roblox have created interactive communities where kids can play with others in real time. These games often involve chat features, virtual economies, and in-game purchases.
- **Streaming and Video Content** – Platforms like YouTube, TikTok, and Netflix are popular among young users for watching educational videos, entertainment clips, and trending challenges. Children consume hours of video content daily, shaping their opinions and interests.
- **Online Learning and Homework Help** – With the growth of digital education, many kids use the internet for school-related activities, virtual learning platforms, and research for homework assignments.
- **Messaging and Communication Apps** – Apps like WhatsApp, Messenger, and Discord allow kids to stay in touch with friends, classmates, and online gaming communities. These apps provide instant communication but also expose children to risks such as online predators and cyberbullying.

Technology provides countless opportunities for learning, creativity, and entertainment, but it also presents new challenges for parents who need to navigate this fast-evolving digital landscape. Understanding where and how kids spend their time online is the first step toward guiding them in making responsible choices.

Common Online Platforms and Their Risks (Social Media, Gaming, Messaging Apps)

Every online platform has its unique features, benefits, and potential risks. Below is a breakdown of some of the most common online spaces that children and teens use today.

1. Social Media Platforms

Social media sites allow children and teenagers to share content, communicate with others, and participate in online trends. Some of the most popular platforms include:

- **TikTok** – A short-video platform that allows users to create and share clips, often featuring music, dances, and challenges. Risk: Exposure to inappropriate content, cyberbullying, and addictive scrolling behavior.
- **Instagram** – A photo and video-sharing app where users post images, stories, and reels. Risk: Pressure to maintain a perfect image, online predators, and the risk of personal data exposure.
- **Snapchat** – A messaging app known for disappearing messages and fun filters. Risk: False sense of security with disappearing messages, cyberbullying, and sexting.

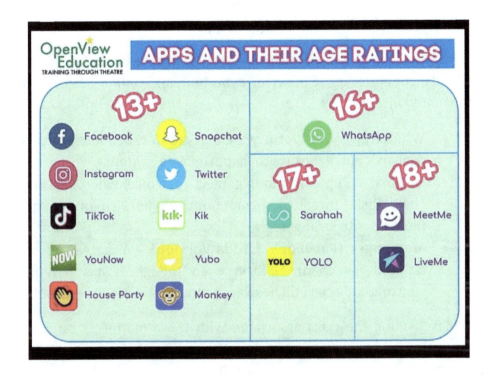

2. Online Gaming Platforms

Many online games have built-in social features, allowing kids to chat and interact with others. Some popular gaming environments include:

- **Roblox** – A platform where users create and play games. Risk: Unregulated chat rooms, in-game purchases, and scams.
- **Fortnite** – A battle royale game with voice and text chat features. Risk: Exposure to strangers, online predators, and gaming addiction.
- **Minecraft** – A creative sandbox game popular among kids. Risk: Interaction with unknown players in multiplayer mode and potential exposure to harmful mods.

3. Messaging and Communication Apps

While messaging apps help children stay connected with family and friends, they also pose risks of cyberbullying, online scams, and unwanted interactions.

- **WhatsApp** – Used for private and group chats. Risk: Privacy concerns and exposure to inappropriate content.
- **Discord** – Popular among gamers for voice, video, and text chats. Risk: Unregulated communities where children might interact with strangers.
- **Messenger (Facebook & Kids Version)** – A messaging app tailored for children. Risk: Even though it has parental controls, kids can still be exposed to risky conversations.

Understanding the risks associated with these platforms can help parents take appropriate measures to ensure their child's online safety.

The Psychological Impact of Digital Exposure on Children

Excessive use of technology and exposure to digital content can have a profound impact on a child's mental and emotional well-being. While technology offers many educational and social benefits, it also comes with psychological risks that parents need to be aware of.

1. Increased Screen Time and Its Effects

Many children spend hours each day using digital devices, often exceeding recommended screen time limits. This can lead to:

- Sleep disturbances due to excessive blue light exposure.
- Reduced physical activity, leading to health issues such as obesity.
- Decreased face-to-face social skills due to reliance on virtual interactions.

2. Social Media and Self-Esteem Issues

Social media platforms often create an unrealistic perception of beauty, success, and happiness. Children and teens may:

- Compare themselves to influencers and celebrities, leading to low self-esteem.
- Feel pressured to gain likes, shares, and followers.
- Experience online bullying or exclusion from social groups.

3. Online Addiction and Its Impact on Mental Health

Some kids develop a dependency on digital platforms, leading to:

- Increased anxiety and depression from overuse.
- A lack of interest in offline activities and hobbies.
- Difficulty concentrating on schoolwork due to constant digital distractions.

4. Exposure to Negative or Harmful Content

Children may accidentally or intentionally come across content that is violent, inappropriate, or misleading. This can:

- Create fear and anxiety about real-world issues.
- Normalize negative behaviors seen in videos or games.
- Influence their beliefs and values in ways parents may not approve of.

Understanding these psychological effects is essential for parents to help their children develop healthy digital habits and maintain a balanced lifestyle.

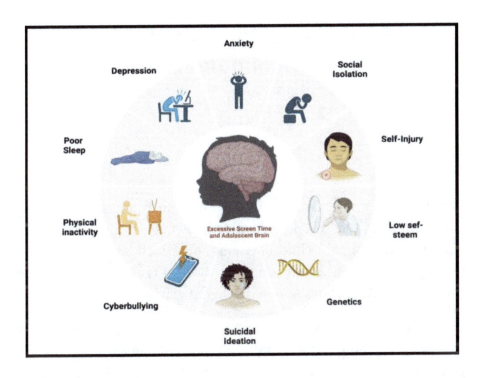

Chapter 2: Cyber Threats Every Parent Should Know

The internet is a vast space filled with opportunities for learning, entertainment, and social connection. However, it also comes with risks that can impact children's emotional well-being, safety, and privacy. As a parent, understanding these threats is the first step toward protecting your child in the digital world.

This chapter will cover the most common online dangers that children face and how they occur. By recognizing these risks early, you can equip your child with the knowledge and tools they need to navigate the internet safely.

Cyberbullying: What It Is and How It Happens

Understanding Cyberbullying

Cyberbullying is the use of digital devices, social media platforms, or online communication tools to harass, humiliate, or intimidate someone. Unlike traditional bullying, which is often limited to school or playgrounds, cyberbullying can happen anytime, anywhere. It follows children into their homes, making it difficult for them to escape the torment.

Cyberbullying can take various forms, including:

- **Harassment:** Sending repeated hurtful or threatening messages.
- **Outing:** Sharing private or embarrassing information without permission.
- **Exclusion:** Deliberately leaving someone out of online groups or activities.
- **Impersonation:** Pretending to be someone else to damage reputations.
- **Trolling:** Posting inflammatory or cruel comments to provoke a reaction.

How Cyberbullying Happens

Children can become victims of cyberbullying through:

- **Social Media** – Hurtful posts, embarrassing pictures, or mean comments.
- **Text Messages & Emails** – Repeated harassment through direct messages.
- **Online Gaming** – Verbal abuse, exclusion from games, or hacking of accounts.
- **Anonymous Apps** – Bullying through anonymous platforms where users hide their identity.

Signs Your Child Might Be a Victim

- Avoids using their phone or computer.
- Becomes withdrawn or anxious after being online.
- Sudden mood swings, frustration, or anger.
- Talks about deleting social media accounts or changing phone numbers.

How Parents Can Help

- **Encourage open communication.** Let your child know they can talk to you if they feel uncomfortable online.
- **Monitor online activity.** Check social media privacy settings and review their interactions.
- **Teach them to block and report.** Show your child how to report abusive users and block cyberbullies.
- **Keep records.** If bullying escalates, save screenshots as evidence and report them to the platform or school authorities.

Online Predators: How They Target Kids

Who Are Online Predators?

Online predators are adults who use the internet to exploit children by forming deceptive relationships. They may pose as peers, gain trust, and manipulate children into inappropriate conversations or dangerous situations.

Where Do They Operate?

- **Social Media Platforms** – They send friend requests or messages pretending to be a child's age.
- **Online Games** – Many predators communicate through in-game chats and voice messages.
- **Messaging Apps** – Platforms like WhatsApp, Discord, or Snapchat allow predators to contact kids directly.
- **Anonymous Chat Rooms** – These platforms provide easy access for predators to talk to children without revealing identities.

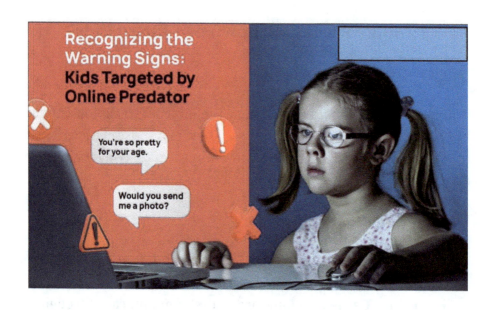

How They Lure Kids

- **Building Trust** – Acting as a friend, liking the same interests, and making the child feel special.
- **Grooming** – Slowly introducing inappropriate topics, asking for secrets, or making children feel guilty.
- **Requesting Personal Information** – Asking for phone numbers, addresses, or school details.
- **Exploiting Curiosity** – Sending inappropriate images or asking children to do the same.

How to Protect Your Child

- **Teach them about online strangers.** Just like in real life, not everyone online is who they claim to be.
- **Monitor friend lists.** Check who they are chatting with online.
- **Enable privacy settings.** Make sure social media accounts are private and not publicly accessible.
- **Encourage them to speak up.** Let them know it's okay to tell you if something feels wrong.

Privacy Risks: The Dangers of Oversharing

Why Oversharing is Dangerous

Children often share too much information online without realizing the risks. Posting photos, locations, or personal details can lead to identity theft, stalking, or cyberbullying.

What Shouldn't Be Shared?

- Full name and birthdate.
- Home address or school name.
- Phone numbers or family details.
- Daily routines or vacation plans.

Steps to Reduce Privacy Risks

- **Set Social Media Accounts to Private.** Ensure only approved friends can see their posts.
- **Review Friend Requests.** Never accept unknown requests.

- **Disable Location Services.** Prevent apps from tracking their location.
- **Think Before Posting.** Teach children to ask themselves if their post is safe to share.

Inappropriate Content: Exposure to Violence, Hate Speech, and Adult Content

Where Kids Encounter Harmful Content

- **YouTube & Streaming Services** – Even with filters, some inappropriate videos may appear.

- **Social Media & Forums** – Harmful images and comments are easily shared.
- **Online Games** – Some games contain violence or unmoderated chatrooms.

How to Keep Kids Safe

- **Use parental controls.** Enable content filters on YouTube, Google, and streaming apps.
- **Encourage safe browsing habits.** Teach them to exit any website that seems inappropriate.
- **Install kid-friendly browsers.** Apps like YouTube Kids provide safer viewing experiences.
- **Have open discussions.** Explain why some content is not suitable for their age.

Scams and Phishing Attacks on Kids

What Are Scams and Phishing Attacks?

Scammers target children through emails, pop-up ads, or fake social media accounts to steal personal information or money.

Common Scams Targeting Kids

- **Fake Giveaways** – "You won an iPhone! Click here!"
- **Phishing Emails** – Pretending to be from a gaming company, asking for passwords.
- **In-Game Scams** – Fake offers for free game currency in exchange for login details.

How Kids Can Avoid Scams

- **Never click suspicious links.** Teach them to ignore pop-ups or unknown messages.
- **Verify before sharing personal info.** Companies will never ask for passwords via email.
- **Report suspicious accounts.** If someone asks for personal data, block and report them.

Final Thoughts

Cyber threats are real, but with awareness and precaution, you can protect your child from online dangers. The key is **education,**

communication, and supervision. By teaching children about these risks, setting boundaries, and monitoring their online activities, you can create a safer digital environment for them.

Part 2: Monitoring & Supervising Your Child's Digital Life

Chapter 3: Setting Digital Boundaries for Kids

Understanding Age-Appropriate Internet Use

In today's digital world, children are introduced to screens and the internet at an early age. While technology offers incredible learning opportunities, entertainment, and communication tools, not all online content is suitable for children. As a parent, it is essential to understand what types of digital activities are appropriate for different age groups. Setting clear, age-appropriate boundaries helps ensure that children develop healthy technology habits while staying safe online.

Why Age-Appropriate Internet Use Matters

Children's cognitive, emotional, and social development progresses through different stages. The way they interact with technology should align with their ability to comprehend and handle online experiences. Younger children are more vulnerable to exposure to harmful content, excessive screen time, and online manipulation. Older children and teens may have more independence online but still require guidance to make responsible choices.

Guidelines for Different Age Groups

Ages 2-5: Early Childhood

- **Screen time should be very limited.** The American Academy of Pediatrics recommends no more than one hour per day of high-quality content.
- **Parental involvement is necessary.** Parents should co-view content, guide interactions, and explain what children see online.
- **No unsupervised internet access.** Children in this age range should only use child-friendly apps and platforms with parental controls enabled.
- **Focus on educational content.** Interactive learning games, storytelling apps, and age-appropriate videos can be beneficial.

Ages 6-9: Early Elementary Years

- **Introduce online safety concepts.** Teach children about privacy, safe searching, and avoiding strangers online.
- **Set time limits.** Aim for no more than 1-2 hours per day of recreational screen time.
- **Encourage creative and educational use.** Apps that promote creativity, such as drawing or coding games, are preferable.
- **Monitor online interactions.** If children use messaging apps or online games, ensure parental controls are in place.

Ages 10-12: Pre-Teen Years

- **Introduce responsible internet use.** Teach kids about digital footprints, online reputation, and appropriate communication.
- **Use parental controls wisely.** Gradually allow more independence while monitoring activity.
- **Encourage a balance of online and offline activities.** Screen-free family time should be emphasized.
- **Start discussing social media.** If children express interest, set guidelines for safe use and ensure privacy settings are enabled.

Ages 13-18: Teenage Years

- **Encourage self-regulation.** Teens should start managing their own screen time with occasional parental guidance.
- **Discuss online risks openly.** Topics like cyberbullying, online predators, and misinformation should be addressed.
- **Set rules for social media use.** Define what is acceptable in terms of sharing content and interacting with others.
- **Promote tech-free zones.** Encourage breaks from technology, especially during meals and before bedtime.

Creating a Family Digital Agreement

A family digital agreement is a contract that outlines rules and expectations regarding technology use. It helps prevent misunderstandings and provides children with a clear framework for responsible online behavior.

Why a Digital Agreement is Important

Children are more likely to follow rules when they are involved in creating them. A digital agreement fosters open communication, ensures consistency in enforcing rules, and allows parents to adapt guidelines as children grow.

Steps to Creating a Family Digital Agreement

Hold a Family Meeting

- Discuss the purpose of the agreement and explain that it is meant to ensure a safe and healthy online experience.
- Allow everyone to share their thoughts and concerns about digital habits.

Set Clear Guidelines

- Define screen time limits for weekdays and weekends.
- Establish rules for using social media, online gaming, and messaging apps.
- Specify acceptable and unacceptable online behavior.

Include Consequences and Rewards

- Outline what happens if rules are broken, such as reduced screen time or loss of device privileges.
- Offer positive reinforcement, like extra screen time for responsible behavior.

Write and Sign the Agreement

- Create a written document that everyone signs as a commitment.
- Post the agreement in a common area as a reminder.

Review and Adjust Regularly

- As children grow and technology changes, revisit and update the agreement.

Establishing Screen Time Limits That Work

Setting screen time limits can be challenging, especially when children use devices for school, entertainment, and socializing. A balanced approach helps maintain healthy habits while still allowing for necessary digital engagement.

How to Set Effective Screen Time Limits

Consider the Purpose of Screen Time

- Differentiate between productive screen time (learning, homework) and recreational screen time (gaming, social media).
- Prioritize educational and creative activities over passive consumption.

Create a Daily or Weekly Plan

- Establish screen-free times, such as during meals and before bedtime.
- Use screen time management tools or apps to enforce limits.

Encourage Alternative Activities

- Promote outdoor play, reading, family interactions, and hobbies.
- Offer incentives for engaging in offline activities.

Lead by Example

- Children mimic parental behavior. Limit your own screen time to set a positive example.

Encouraging a Healthy Online-Offline Balance

A healthy relationship with technology involves knowing when to unplug and engage in real-world experiences. Parents play a key role in fostering this balance.

Strategies to Maintain a Digital-Real Life Balance

Designate Tech-Free Zones

- No screens during meals, family gatherings, or bedtime.
- Create screen-free spaces in the house, such as bedrooms.

Encourage Outdoor and Physical Activities

- Plan family outings that do not involve screens.
- Promote sports, exercise, and nature activities.

Set a Good Example

- Show enthusiasm for offline activities.
- Avoid excessive phone use in front of children.

Encourage Social Interaction Without Screens

- Arrange playdates, family game nights, and community activities.
- Foster face-to-face conversations over digital messaging.

Help Children Develop Offline Hobbies

- Encourage reading, arts and crafts, music, or other creative pursuits.
- Support activities that build skills outside of digital devices.

By implementing these strategies, families can create a digital environment that supports learning, entertainment, and connection while ensuring that screen time remains balanced with real-world experiences. The goal is not to eliminate technology but to teach children how to use it responsibly and in moderation.

Chapter 4: Parental Controls & Monitoring Tools

Setting Up Parental Controls on Devices and Apps

Understanding Parental Controls

Parental controls are tools that help you manage what your child can access on their devices, apps, and the internet. These controls allow you to filter content, set time limits, restrict purchases, and monitor usage to ensure a safe digital environment for your child. Many devices and applications have built-in parental controls that you can customize based on your child's age and needs.

Using parental controls does not mean you don't trust your child. Instead, it provides a safety net that protects them from inappropriate content, online predators, and digital addiction. Think of it as the online equivalent of ensuring your child wears a seatbelt while in a car.

How to Set Up Parental Controls on Common Devices

1. Smartphones and Tablets (iOS & Android)

Most smartphones and tablets have built-in settings that allow parents to control and restrict their child's activity.

For iPhones and iPads (iOS):

- Open **Settings** and tap on **Screen Time**.
- Tap **Turn On Screen Time**, then select **This is My Child's iPhone/iPad**.
- Set up **Downtime** (to limit device usage during specific hours).
- Use **App Limits** to restrict time spent on certain apps.
- Enable **Content & Privacy Restrictions** to block inappropriate content and control privacy settings.
- Set up **Ask to Buy** for purchases, so your child must request permission before making purchases.

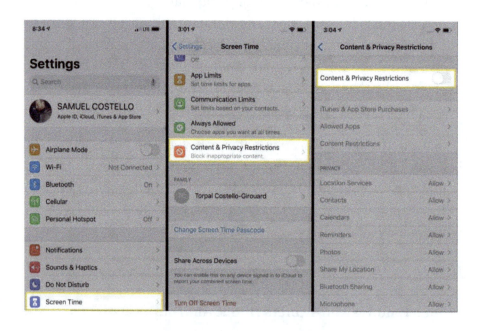

For Android Devices:

- Open **Google Play Store** and tap on the **Profile icon.**
- Select **Family > Parental Controls.**
- Toggle **Parental Controls On** and set up a PIN.
- Adjust settings for apps, games, movies, and TV based on age ratings.
- Use **Google Family Link** (a free app) to monitor and control your child's device remotely.

2. Gaming Consoles (PlayStation, Xbox, Nintendo Switch)

Many children spend hours gaming, so setting up parental controls on gaming consoles is just as important as on other devices.

PlayStation:

- Go to **Settings > Parental Controls/Family Management.**
- Create a **Child Account.**
- Set restrictions for playtime, content rating, and online interactions.

Xbox:

- Open **Settings > Account > Family Settings.**
- Add your child's account and adjust restrictions.
- Enable **screen time limits and purchase restrictions.**

Nintendo Switch:

- Download the **Nintendo Switch Parental Controls app.**
- Link it to your child's console.
- Set time limits, content restrictions, and online communication controls.

3. Smart TVs and Streaming Services (Netflix, YouTube, Disney+)

Children have easy access to smart TVs and streaming platforms, so it's essential to set up restrictions.

- **Netflix:** Enable **Kid Profiles** with age-appropriate content.
- **YouTube:** Turn on **Restricted Mode** to filter out harmful videos.
- **Disney+:** Use **Parental Profiles** to block mature content.
- **How to Use Built-in Safety Features (YouTube, Google, iOS, Android)**

YouTube's Safety Features

YouTube is one of the most popular platforms among children, but it also contains inappropriate content. Here's how to make YouTube safer for your child:

Turn on Restricted Mode:

- Open **YouTube**.
- Tap on **Profile Picture > Settings**.
- Enable **Restricted Mode** to filter out explicit content.

Use YouTube Kids:

- Download **YouTube Kids**, a safer version for children.
- Set up profiles based on age (Preschool, Younger, Older).
- Monitor watch history and block unwanted videos.

Google SafeSearch and Family Link

Google's search engine can expose children to harmful content. SafeSearch filters explicit results, while Family Link gives parents full control over their child's Google account.

Turn on SafeSearch:

- Go to **Google Search Settings**.
- Enable **SafeSearch Filters**.

Use Family Link:

- Download **Google Family Link**.
- Link it to your child's Google account.
- Set limits on app usage, location tracking, and content restrictions.

iOS and Android Safety Settings

- **iOS:** Use **Screen Time** to set app limits and privacy restrictions.
- **Android:** Use **Family Link** for monitoring and app restrictions.

Monitoring Apps: The Pros and Cons

Why Use a Monitoring App?

Monitoring apps give parents insight into their child's digital activity, helping them detect risks early. However, they come with advantages and disadvantages.

Pros:

- **Real-time Monitoring** – Track your child's internet activity and location.
- **Content Filtering** – Block inappropriate content.
- **App Usage Reports** – See which apps your child uses most.
- **Screen Time Control** – Set time limits on specific apps.

Cons:

- **Privacy Concerns** – Children may feel their privacy is violated.
- **Trust Issues** – Over-monitoring can damage parent-child trust.
- **Potential Workarounds** – Tech-savvy kids may bypass restrictions.

Popular Monitoring Apps

- **Bark** – Monitors text messages, social media, and online searches.
- **Qustodio** – Tracks screen time, filters content, and monitors calls.
- **Norton Family** – Helps parents monitor and block harmful websites.

- **Google Family Link** – Best for managing Android devices.

Tracking Online Activity Without Violating Trust

How to Monitor Without Spying

Monitoring should not feel like spying. Instead, approach it as a way to educate and protect your child. Here's how to do it respectfully:

- **Have an Open Conversation** – Explain why monitoring is important and set clear boundaries.
- **Set Expectations Together** – Create a Family Digital Agreement outlining rules.
- **Encourage Self-Regulation** – Teach children to make responsible choices online.
- **Gradual Independence** – Adjust controls as your child grows and earns trust.

Signs That Monitoring is Needed

- Sudden changes in mood or secrecy about device usage.
- Excessive screen time and withdrawal from family activities.
- Strange messages or interactions with unknown individuals online.

Balancing Safety and Trust

The goal of parental controls and monitoring is not to control every aspect of your child's digital life but to provide a **safe, structured environment** where they can explore the internet responsibly. By combining **technology, open communication, and guidance**, you can help your child develop **healthy digital habits** while keeping them protected from online dangers.

With the right tools, settings, and conversations, you can create a **secure online environment** for your child without restricting their ability to **learn, connect, and grow** in the digital world.

Chapter 5: Safe Social Media and Messaging Practices

The world of social media is a fascinating, engaging, and sometimes overwhelming space for children and teenagers. It allows them to connect with friends, share experiences, and express themselves. However, as with any online platform, there are risks, including privacy concerns, cyberbullying, scams, and exposure to inappropriate content.

As a parent, your role is to guide and equip your child with the right knowledge and skills to navigate social media safely. In this chapter, we will explore popular social media platforms, discuss how to set privacy settings, recognize fake accounts and scams, and prevent cyberbullying.

Popular Social Media Platforms (Instagram, Snapchat, TikTok, Discord)

Before diving into safety measures, it's important to understand the most commonly used social media platforms among children and teens. Each platform has its own features, benefits, and risks. Below is a breakdown of some of the most popular ones:

Instagram

Instagram is a photo and video-sharing app where users can post content, interact with others, and send private messages (DMs). The platform is widely used by teens and young adults.

- **Key Features:** Stories, reels, IG Live, direct messaging, and comment sections.
- **Potential Risks:** Privacy concerns, cyberbullying, exposure to inappropriate content, and pressure to maintain a 'perfect' online image.

Snapchat

Snapchat is a messaging app where photos and videos (called snaps) disappear after being viewed. The app also features Stories, Streaks, and private messaging.

- **Key Features:** Disappearing messages, Snap Map (location sharing), and filters.
- **Potential Risks:** Screenshot risks, disappearing messages can create a false sense of security, and location tracking.

TikTok

TikTok is a short-form video-sharing app where users create and watch entertaining content. It is widely popular among kids and teens.

- **Key Features:** Trending challenges, duets, live streaming, and an interactive comment section.
- **Potential Risks:** Exposure to inappropriate content, cyberbullying in comments, and interaction with strangers.

Discord

Discord is a communication platform used primarily by gamers but also by online communities.

- **Key Features:** Voice chats, group messaging, and community servers.
- **Potential Risks:** Exposure to adult content, communication with strangers, and unmoderated chatrooms.

Understanding these platforms allows parents to have informed discussions with their children about potential risks and how to stay safe.

Setting Privacy Settings and Restrictions

One of the best ways to protect your child online is by ensuring they have the right privacy settings on their social media accounts. Most platforms have built-in privacy features that allow users to control who can see their posts, send them messages, and interact with their content.

Steps to Set Privacy Settings on Social Media

Switch Accounts to Private Mode:

- On Instagram, TikTok, and Snapchat, you can set the account to private so only approved followers can see content.
- On Discord, ensure direct messages are restricted to friends only.

Turn Off Location Sharing:

- Apps like Snapchat and Instagram have location-sharing features. Disable these settings to protect your child's privacy.

Limit Who Can Contact Your Child:

- Adjust settings so only friends can send direct messages or comment on posts.

Enable Content Restrictions:

- Use built-in content filters to block inappropriate videos and images on TikTok and Instagram.

Monitor App Permissions:

- Check what permissions each app has (camera, microphone, location) and disable anything unnecessary.
- Taking these steps will help create a safer online experience for your child.

Teaching Kids to Recognize Fake Accounts and Scams

Not everyone on social media is who they claim to be. Scammers, hackers, and online predators often create fake accounts to deceive users. Teaching kids how to recognize and avoid these threats is crucial.

How to Identify a Fake Account

- **Check the Profile Picture and Bio:** Fake accounts often use stock images or stolen photos. If an account has no bio, no profile picture, or only a few generic posts, it may be fake.
- **Look at the Follower-to-Following Ratio:** Fake accounts often have a very low number of followers but follow thousands of people.
- **Analyze the Messages:** If someone sends a random message claiming they "won a prize" or requests personal information, it's likely a scam.
- **Watch for Phishing Attempts:** Fake accounts may send links that lead to harmful websites asking for login credentials. Teach children never to click on suspicious links.
- **Verify Friends and Followers:** Encourage children to only accept friend requests from people they know in real life.

How to Spot and Prevent Cyberbullying

Cyberbullying is a serious issue that can have long-term emotional and psychological effects on children. Unlike traditional bullying, cyberbullying follows kids into their homes through their screens, making it harder to escape.

Signs That Your Child Might Be Experiencing Cyberbullying

- They become withdrawn or anxious after using their phone.
- They suddenly stop using certain apps or social media platforms.
- They appear upset or angry after being online.
- They avoid talking about their online interactions.

Steps to Prevent and Address Cyberbullying

- **Encourage Open Communication:** Let your child know they can always talk to you about anything that happens online.
- **Teach Them to Block and Report Bullies:** Show them how to block and report harmful users on social media platforms.

- **Save Evidence of Cyberbullying:** If your child receives harmful messages or comments, take screenshots before blocking the user.
- **Set Up Monitoring Tools:** Use parental controls and monitoring apps to stay informed about your child's online activity.
- **Promote Positive Online Behavior:** Encourage kids to be kind online and avoid engaging in negative interactions.
- **Know When to Seek Help:** If cyberbullying escalates, report it to the school, platform moderators, or even law enforcement if necessary.

Final Thoughts

Social media can be a fun and safe place for kids if used correctly. By understanding the risks, setting up proper privacy settings, teaching children to recognize fake accounts, and addressing cyberbullying, parents can create a safer online environment.

The most important thing is to maintain an open dialogue with your child. Encourage them to ask questions, share concerns, and come to you whenever they feel uncomfortable online. With the right guidance and education, they can enjoy social media while staying safe from potential threats.

Part 3: Educating and Empowering Your Child

Chapter 6: Teaching Kids About Online Safety

The internet is an incredible place filled with opportunities for learning, entertainment, and communication. However, it also has risks that children must learn to navigate safely. As parents, our role is not just to block dangers but to equip our kids with the knowledge and skills to protect themselves.

In this chapter, we will explore how to talk to kids about internet dangers in a way that empowers rather than frightens them. We will also cover how to help children recognize and handle cyberbullying, how to discuss online predators in an age-appropriate way, and how to develop critical thinking skills to evaluate online content.

By the end of this chapter, you will have practical strategies for guiding your children toward responsible and safe internet use while building a trusting and open dialogue with them.

The Right Way to Talk About Internet Dangers

Talking to kids about online dangers can be tricky. If you scare them too much, they might avoid coming to you for help. If you make it seem unimportant, they might not take safety seriously. The key is to **strike a balance**—educate them about risks while reinforcing that they can make smart, safe choices with the right knowledge.

Start With Open Conversations

Before jumping into rules and warnings, first, understand what your child already knows. Ask them:

- "What do you like to do online?"
- "Have you ever seen anything online that made you uncomfortable?"
- "How do you decide if something is safe on the internet?"

Listen carefully to their responses. This will give you insight into their level of awareness and help tailor your guidance.

Use Everyday Examples

Children understand real-life situations better than abstract threats. Instead of saying, *"Strangers on the internet are dangerous,"* say:

- *"Imagine if a stranger walked up to you on the street and asked for your name and address. Would you give it to them?"*
- *"If someone at the park kept following you and saying things that made you uncomfortable, what would you do?"*

Once they grasp the real-world example, relate it to the internet:

- *"The same rules apply online. If someone you don't know asks for personal information, don't share it."*

Encourage Questions and Make It a Two-Way Conversation

Your child should feel comfortable asking questions, even about things they might feel embarrassed or unsure about. Let them know it's okay to talk to you if something online makes them feel **weird, scared, or uncomfortable**—without fear of punishment.

Reassure them with statements like:

- *"I'm here to help you, not to get you in trouble."*
- *"No matter what happens online, you can always talk to me."*

This builds trust and makes them more likely to seek your help when needed.

Teach Your Kids About

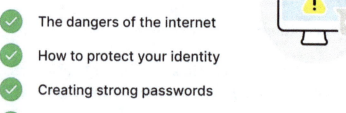

- ✓ The dangers of the internet
- ✓ How to protect your identity
- ✓ Creating strong passwords
- ✓ Not engaging with strangers in person or online
- ✓ Keeping social media accounts private
- ✓ Being careful about what they post

Teaching Kids to Identify and Handle Cyberbullying

Cyberbullying is one of the most common online dangers kids face. It includes mean messages, spreading rumors, embarrassing photos, or exclusion from online groups.

Helping Kids Recognize Cyberbullying

Explain that cyberbullying is any online behavior that is:

- **Hurtful** – Insulting, mocking, or making someone feel bad.
- **Repeated** – It happens more than once or is meant to humiliate.
- **Intentional** – It is done to make someone feel upset.

Ask questions like:

- "How do you think it feels to be bullied online?"
- "Have you ever seen someone being mean to another person online?"

Encourage empathy by discussing how they would feel if the situation were reversed.

Steps to Handle Cyberbullying

- **Ignore minor incidents** – If it's a one-time mean comment, sometimes the best response is no response.
- **Block and report the bully** – Show them how to block users and report harmful content.
- **Save evidence** – Take screenshots in case the bullying escalates.
- **Tell a trusted adult** – Let them know they don't have to deal with it alone.
- **Support friends** – Encourage them to stand up for others who are being bullied.

How to Talk About Online Predators Without Scaring Them

Online predators often disguise themselves to befriend children and gain their trust. However, children should not live in constant fear. Instead, they should **know the warning signs** and how to protect themselves.

Teach the Concept of Online Strangers

Use simple comparisons:

- *"Not everyone online is who they say they are, just like in real life."*
- *"Would you trust a random person who walks up and says they are your new best friend?"*

Explain that online strangers may try to:

- Ask for personal information (address, phone number, school name).
- Offer gifts or prizes to lure them in.
- Make them keep secrets from their parents.
- Ask them to send pictures or meet in person.

What to Do if Someone Seems Suspicious

- **Never respond** – Teach them to ignore and block strangers.
- **Don't share personal details** – Even small details like school name can be risky.
- **Tell an adult immediately** – Always report suspicious behavior.

Role-play different scenarios so they can practice how to respond safely.

Encouraging Critical Thinking About Online Content

Not everything on the internet is true. Misinformation, scams, and harmful content are everywhere. Kids must learn to question and analyze what they see online.

Teach Them to Spot Fake News and Clickbait

Show examples of:

- Sensational headlines (*"This Magic Pill Can Make You Fly!"*)
- Edited images (*"A celebrity seen in two places at once"*)
- False social media claims (*"Share this to get free money!"*)

Encourage them to ask:

- "Who wrote this? Can I trust them?"
- "Where did this information come from?"
- "Is this trying to trick me into clicking?"

Discuss the Influence of Social Media

Talk about how influencers and ads shape opinions. Ask:

- "Do you think everything influencers say is real?"
- "Why do companies want us to believe their product is the best?"

Encouraging these questions helps children develop a **healthy skepticism** and make informed choices.

Conclusion: Empowering Kids to Be Smart Digital Citizens

Teaching online safety is not about creating fear but about empowering kids with **knowledge and confidence**. By having open discussions, setting clear guidelines, and reinforcing critical thinking skills, we prepare them to make safe choices online.

The goal is to raise children who are:

- **Aware** of online risks.
- **Confident** in handling difficult situations.
- **Comfortable** discussing online concerns with trusted adults.

By staying engaged and guiding them through the digital world, we give them the best tools to navigate it safely and responsibly.

Chapter 7: Digital Footprint & Online Reputation

What Is a Digital Footprint?

Imagine walking along a sandy beach. Every step you take leaves a footprint behind. Even if the waves wash some away, others remain imprinted in the sand. The internet works the same way. Every time you or your child interacts online—whether posting a photo, leaving a comment, liking a video, or even searching for something—it leaves a digital trace. This collection of traces is known as a **digital footprint**.

A digital footprint is the record of everything a person does on the internet. It includes social media activity, browsing history, shared content, and even interactions with websites and apps. Some parts of a digital footprint are **active**, meaning they are intentionally created, such as a social media post. Others are **passive**, meaning they are collected without the user's direct involvement, such as cookies tracking browsing habits or search engines storing past searches.

Many parents assume that what their child does online is temporary, but in reality, digital footprints are often **permanent**. Even if something is deleted, copies might still exist somewhere on the internet. Screenshots, archived pages, or saved downloads can make information last far beyond its intended lifespan. This is why it is

crucial to educate children about their digital footprint early so they understand the long-term impact of their online actions.

How Kids' Online Actions Affect Their Future

Children and teenagers may not fully understand that their online behavior can shape their future. What seems like a harmless joke today could resurface years later when applying for college, a scholarship, or a job. Schools, employers, and even potential friends or partners often look at a person's digital presence to learn more about them.

Here are a few ways a digital footprint can impact the future:

1. College Admissions

Many universities now review applicants' social media and online activity as part of their evaluation process. A student with inappropriate content, offensive comments, or evidence of irresponsible behavior might lose their chance at admission. Conversely, a positive online presence—such as sharing achievements, volunteer work, or insightful content—can leave a good impression.

2. Employment Opportunities

Hiring managers often look at social media profiles before making hiring decisions. If a candidate has a history of sharing negative, reckless, or unprofessional content, they may be seen as a risk to the company. On the other hand, a digital footprint showcasing professionalism, skills, and responsibility can give an applicant a strong advantage.

3. Reputation and Relationships

Beyond academics and careers, digital footprints shape personal relationships. A child who bullies others online or shares offensive content could damage friendships and even face social consequences in school. A positive online reputation, built on kindness, respect, and responsibility, helps in maintaining strong, healthy relationships.

4. Online Security Risks

Hackers, scammers, and online predators often target individuals based on their digital footprint. If children overshare personal details, such as their location, school name, or daily routines, they could become victims of identity theft, scams, or cyberstalking. Teaching them to be cautious about what they reveal online can significantly reduce these risks.

The Risks of Posting Personal Information

One of the most common mistakes children and teenagers make is **oversharing personal information online**. They may not realize that sharing certain details can expose them to cyber threats or long-term consequences. Here are some key risks:

1. Identity Theft

Even seemingly harmless details—like a birth date, phone number, or home address—can be used by cybercriminals to steal someone's identity. With enough information, criminals can impersonate someone, open bank accounts in their name, or even commit fraud.

2. Privacy Invasion

Once personal details are shared, they can be difficult to control. A simple social media post about a vacation could alert burglars that a house is empty. A child sharing their school name could make them an easy target for online predators.

3. Cyberbullying and Harassment

Sharing personal photos, opinions, or life updates makes children more vulnerable to cyberbullying. Strangers or even classmates may take their content out of context, spread rumors, or use information to harm them emotionally.

4. Permanent Online Record

The internet does not forget. Even if a post is deleted, it may already be saved by someone else. Screenshots, backups, or archived web pages can ensure that once something is posted, it exists forever.

How Can Parents Help?

- Teach children to **never** share their full name, address, school, or phone number online.
- Encourage them to use **privacy settings** on all social media accounts.
- Explain why sharing their **location in real-time** can be dangerous.
- Remind them that even trusted friends can **accidentally or intentionally** spread private information.

Teaching Kids to Think Before They Share

One of the best ways to protect a child's online reputation is to teach them **critical thinking before posting anything online**. A simple rule to follow is: **"Would I be okay if this were seen by my teacher, future boss, or grandmother?"** If the answer is no, it's better not to share it.

Here are some **guidelines** children can use before sharing online:

1. The T.H.I.N.K. Rule

Before posting, ask:

- **T** – Is it **True**? (Avoid spreading false information.)
- **H** – Is it **Helpful**? (Does it add value to others?)
- **I** – Is it **Inspiring**? (Does it encourage positive actions?)
- **N** – Is it **Necessary**? (Does it really need to be shared?)
- **K** – Is it **Kind**? (Would it hurt someone's feelings?)

2. The 24-Hour Rule

If unsure about posting something, **wait 24 hours** before making it public. This gives time to reflect on whether the content is appropriate and necessary.

3. Check Privacy Settings Regularly

Social media platforms update their settings frequently. Children should check their privacy settings at least once every few months to ensure only trusted people can see their posts.

4. Avoid Sharing When Emotional

People often regret posting when they are angry, upset, or frustrated. Teach children to **pause before posting**, especially if they feel emotional.

5. Be Mindful of Tagged Content

Even if a child does not post something themselves, **friends can tag them in photos or comments**. They should regularly check their tagged content and untag themselves from anything inappropriate.

6. Think Beyond the Screen

Remind kids that **their online actions reflect who they are in real life**. Whether applying for a job, making new friends, or building a personal brand, their online reputation plays a big role in how others perceive them.

Conclusion

A digital footprint is like an **online diary** that follows children into adulthood. It can either be a **powerful tool for success** or a **risk to their future**. By teaching kids how their online actions affect their future, the risks of oversharing, and the importance of **thinking before sharing**, parents can help them build a **positive and safe digital reputation**.

Encourage children to see the internet as a **place of opportunity**, but also as a **space where responsibility matters**. By developing smart online habits today, they can ensure a **bright and secure future in the digital world**.

Chapter 8: Safe Online Gaming for Kids

Gaming has become a huge part of children's entertainment, with millions of kids worldwide engaging in online multiplayer games. While gaming can be fun, interactive, and even educational, it also comes with certain risks that parents must understand and address. In this chapter, we will explore the potential dangers of online gaming, how to set safe boundaries, how to recognize and avoid scams, and how to choose age-appropriate games for children.

The Risks of Online Gaming (Chat Rooms, Micro transactions, Addiction)

1. Chat Rooms and Online Interactions

Many online games include chat features that allow players to communicate with one another. While this can encourage teamwork and social interaction, it also opens the door to potential risks:

- **Inappropriate Language and Content:** Some chat rooms are unmoderated, exposing children to offensive language, bullying, or inappropriate discussions.

- **Strangers and Online Predators:** Not everyone in an online game is who they claim to be. Predators can pose as friendly gamers to build trust and exploit children.
- **Personal Information Risks:** Children may unknowingly share sensitive information such as their real name, location, or school details, which can put them in danger.

2. Microtransactions and In-Game Purchases

Many online games offer additional content through microtransactions, which allow players to buy virtual goods such as character outfits, weapons, or special abilities. While these purchases may seem harmless, they can lead to:

- **Excessive Spending:** Some games encourage impulse purchases, leading kids to spend large amounts of money without understanding the real-world cost.
- **Hidden Charges:** Some games require linking to a credit card, which could lead to unauthorized purchases.
- **Pay-to-Win Mechanics:** Some games give paying players unfair advantages, pushing children to feel pressured to spend money to compete.

3. Gaming Addiction and Excessive Screen Time

Games are designed to be engaging and rewarding, which can sometimes lead to excessive play. The risks of gaming addiction include:

- **Neglecting Responsibilities:** Kids may prioritize gaming over schoolwork, chores, and family time.
- **Lack of Sleep and Physical Activity:** Late-night gaming sessions can lead to sleep deprivation, while long hours in

front of a screen can reduce physical activity and impact overall health.

- **Emotional Dependence:** Some children may become overly attached to their gaming identities and experiences, leading to frustration and anger when unable to play.

Setting Boundaries for Safe Gaming

To ensure a healthy gaming experience, parents should establish clear boundaries and guidelines. Here's how:

1. Establish Screen Time Limits

- **Set daily or weekly gaming limits** to ensure a balanced lifestyle. A good rule is no more than 1-2 hours of gaming on school days and 2-3 hours on weekends.
- Use built-in parental controls on gaming consoles and devices to automatically limit playtime.

2. Create a Gaming Schedule

- Encourage gaming only **after homework and chores** are completed.
- Designate **gaming-free zones**, such as during meals or before bedtime, to prevent excessive screen time.

3. Keep Gaming in a Shared Space

- Have children play in common areas where parents can monitor activity.
- Avoid allowing gaming in bedrooms to reduce the risk of late-night play and exposure to unmonitored content.

4. Encourage Open Communication

- Talk to your child about their gaming experiences. Ask about their favorite games, who they interact with, and if they've encountered any problems.
- Teach them to **report any inappropriate behavior** they witness or experience online.

Recognizing and Avoiding In-Game Scams and Predators

Many scams and online threats exist in the gaming world, and children should be aware of how to recognize and avoid them.

1. Common In-Game Scams

- **Fake Giveaways:** Scammers may offer "free" game items in exchange for personal information or access to accounts.
- **Phishing Links:** Suspicious links in chat messages can lead to fake websites designed to steal login credentials.
- **Account Hacking:** Fraudulent messages may trick players into sharing their passwords, leading to stolen accounts.

2. How to Stay Safe from Scams

- **Never Share Login Information:** Teach children to keep their usernames, passwords, and personal details private.
- **Use Two-Factor Authentication (2FA):** Many games offer 2FA to protect accounts from being hacked.
- **Be Skeptical of Unsolicited Messages:** If someone offers free in-game items, it's likely a scam.

3. Avoiding Online Predators

- **Never Add or Chat with Strangers:** Explain the risks of befriending unknown players online.
- **Use Private or Friends-Only Chats:** Most games allow players to limit chat interactions to approved friends.
- **Report Suspicious Behavior:** If someone makes inappropriate requests or behaves strangely, report and block them immediately.

Selecting Age-Appropriate Games

Not all games are suitable for children. Parents should carefully select games that align with their child's age and maturity level.

1. Check Game Ratings

- **Use the ESRB (Entertainment Software Rating Board) or PEGI (Pan European Game Information) ratings** to determine if a game is appropriate for your child's age.
- **Avoid games with excessive violence, strong language, or mature content.**

2. Research the Game Before Allowing Play

- Read game reviews and **watch gameplay videos** to understand the game's content.
- Use websites like **Common Sense Media** for detailed breakdowns of a game's risks and benefits.

3. Choose Games with Educational or Social Benefits

- Look for games that promote **problem-solving, creativity, and teamwork.**
- Examples of safe, educational, and fun games for kids include **Minecraft, Animal Crossing, and Super Mario games.**

4. Set Up Parental Controls

- Many gaming consoles and platforms allow parents to **restrict game purchases, chat features, and screen time.**
- Enable content filters to block access to mature or inappropriate games.

Conclusion

Online gaming can be a safe and enjoyable activity for kids when proper precautions are taken. By understanding the risks, setting clear gaming boundaries, teaching children about scams and online predators, and selecting age-appropriate games, parents can ensure that their child's gaming experience is positive and secure. The key is **maintaining open communication** and **regularly monitoring gaming habits** to create a healthy balance between digital play and other life activities.

By following these guidelines, parents can empower their children to enjoy gaming safely while developing responsible digital habits.

Part 4: Protecting Your Child from Cyber Threats

Chapter 9: Cybersecurity Basics for Families

The internet is a powerful tool that connects us to a world of information, communication, and entertainment. However, just like the real world, it comes with risks. Cybercriminals are always looking for ways to steal personal information, hack accounts, and trick people into revealing sensitive data. As a parent, one of your biggest responsibilities in digital parenting is to ensure your family follows **strong cybersecurity practices** to stay safe online.

This chapter will guide you through the essentials of cybersecurity for families, including how to **create strong passwords, use two-factor authentication, practice safe browsing, avoid scams and phishing attacks, and handle a hacked account.** By following these steps, you can significantly reduce the risks of cyber threats and protect your family's personal information.

Creating Strong Passwords and Using Two-Factor Authentication

The Importance of Strong Passwords

Passwords are the first line of defense against hackers and cybercriminals. Weak or easily guessed passwords can put your entire online identity at risk. Many people use passwords that are too simple, like "123456," "password," or their birthdate, making it easy for attackers to break into their accounts.

To create a strong password, follow these key guidelines:

- **How to Create a Strong Password**
- **Make It Long** – Use at least **12–16 characters** or more.
- **Mix Upper and Lowercase Letters** – This makes it harder to guess.
- **Use Numbers and Symbols** – A good password includes a mix of letters, numbers, and special characters (*, @, $, %, etc.).
- **Avoid Personal Information** – Do not use names, birthdays, or words related to your family.
- **Never Reuse Passwords** – Each account should have a unique password.
- **Use Passphrases** – Instead of a single word, use a phrase like **"Sunny$Beach8!RainyDay"** for better security.
- **Consider a Password Manager** – A **password manager** can store and generate complex passwords so you don't have to remember them all.

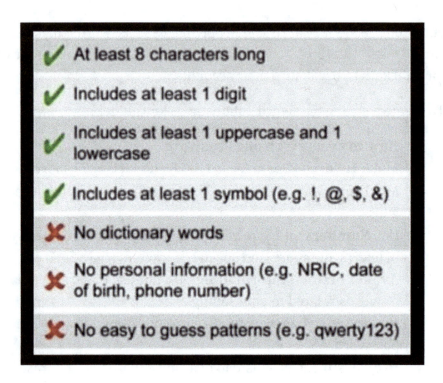

Two-Factor Authentication (2FA): Adding an Extra Layer of Security

Even with a strong password, accounts can still be compromised. **Two-Factor Authentication (2FA)** adds another layer of security by requiring a second form of verification, such as:

- A **one-time code** sent to your phone or email.
- A **fingerprint scan** or facial recognition.
- A **security key** or authentication app.

How to Enable Two-Factor Authentication

- **Go to Account Settings** – Find the security settings in the app or website.
- **Look for 2FA or Two-Step Verification** – This option is usually under "Security."
- **Choose Your Method** – Select whether you want to receive codes via SMS, email, or authentication app.
- **Confirm and Save** – Follow the steps to activate it and test it to make sure it works.

Encourage your children to **enable 2FA on their accounts** as well. Even if someone steals their password, they won't be able to access the account without the second authentication step.

Safe Browsing Practices for Kids

Why Safe Browsing Matters

The internet is full of useful information, but it also has harmful websites, fake news, and cyber threats. Kids may accidentally click on dangerous links or enter unsafe websites without realizing the risks. Teaching safe browsing habits helps protect them from inappropriate content, malware, and cybercriminals.

Tips for Safe Internet Browsing

- **Use Child-Friendly Browsers** – Set up browsers like **Google SafeSearch, Kiddle, or YouTube Kids** to filter out harmful content.
- **Enable Safe Browsing Mode** – Most browsers have a **"Safe Browsing"** setting that blocks dangerous websites.

- **Teach Kids to Recognize Secure Websites** – Look for the **lock icon (🔒)** in the address bar and ensure the URL starts with **"https://"** (not "http://").
- **Warn About Pop-Up Ads and Fake Links** – Teach kids never to click on strange pop-ups or links from unknown sources.
- **Use Parental Controls** – Set up parental controls on devices to **block access to inappropriate websites.**
- **Limit Downloads** – Tell kids to always ask before downloading apps, games, or files.

Avoiding Scams and Phishing Attacks

What Are Scams and Phishing Attacks?

Scams and phishing attacks trick people into giving away personal information, passwords, or financial details. Cybercriminals use fake emails, messages, or websites to **pretend to be someone trustworthy**, such as a bank, a game developer, or a friend.

How to Spot a Phishing Scam

- **Look for Suspicious Emails or Messages** – If an email says "Your account has been hacked! Click here to fix it," it's likely fake.
- **Check the Sender's Email Address** – Scammers often use email addresses that look like real ones but have small differences.
- **Never Click on Unknown Links** – Always hover over links before clicking to see where they lead.
- **Beware of Urgent or Scary Messages** – Scammers try to scare you into acting fast.
- **Avoid Sharing Personal Information** – Never enter passwords, credit card details, or personal info in emails or messages.
- **Use Anti-Phishing Tools** – Many browsers and email services offer built-in protection against phishing attempts.

What to Do If You or Your Child Falls for a Scam

- **Do not respond** to the message or email.
- **Change passwords immediately** if an account is compromised.

- **Enable 2FA** to add extra security.
- **Check account activity** for unauthorized logins or transactions.
- **Report the scam** to the website, platform, or law enforcement if needed.

How to Handle a Hacked Account

Signs That an Account Has Been Hacked

- You can't log in because the password has changed.
- You see **strange activity** (messages you didn't send, posts you didn't make).
- Friends receive weird messages from your account.
- You get security alerts or emails about **login attempts from unknown locations.**

Steps to Recover a Hacked Account

- **Try to Log In and Change Your Password**
- If you can access the account, **immediately change the password** to a stronger one.
- **Use Password Recovery Options.** Click on "Forgot Password?" and follow the instructions to reset it.
- **Enable Two-Factor Authentication.** If not already enabled, turn on **2FA** to prevent future hacks.
- **Check and Remove Unknown Devices.** Go to the account settings and **log out of unfamiliar devices**.
- **Report the Hack to the Platform.** Contact customer support (Google, Facebook, etc.) for assistance.

- **Warn Friends and Family**. Tell them not to open suspicious messages or links from your account.
- **Scan for Malware**. Run a virus scan on all devices to check for keyloggers or malware.

By following these steps, you can **regain control** of your account and prevent further damage.

Final Thoughts

Cybersecurity is an ongoing process, and digital safety should be a **family effort**. Teaching kids to recognize online threats, use strong passwords, browse safely, and avoid scams will **empower them to navigate the internet securely**. Make these cybersecurity practices a habit, and you'll create a safer digital environment for your entire family.

Chapter 10: Dealing with Cyberbullying

The internet is a space where children and teens connect, learn, and express themselves. However, it also exposes them to risks, one of the most serious being cyberbullying. Unlike traditional bullying, which happens face-to-face, cyberbullying takes place online—through social media, messaging apps, emails, and gaming platforms. It can feel relentless because digital content spreads quickly and can be difficult to erase.

As a parent, guardian, or educator, understanding cyberbullying and knowing how to address it is crucial for protecting children. This chapter will guide you through recognizing signs of cyberbullying, responding effectively, and taking necessary actions to ensure your child's safety and emotional well-being.

How to Spot Signs Your Child is Being Cyberbullied

Many children do not openly discuss cyberbullying because they fear embarrassment, retaliation, or that their devices will be taken away. This makes it important to recognize behavioral and emotional signs that may indicate your child is being targeted. Here are some key indicators:

Behavioral Changes:

- **Avoidance of Devices:** If your child suddenly stops using their phone, tablet, or computer, it may be because they are receiving distressing messages online.
- **Nervousness When Online:** If they appear anxious or upset when receiving notifications, they might be experiencing cyberbullying.
- **Withdrawal from Social Activities:** If your child loses interest in socializing, even with close friends, it could be due to online harassment.
- **Changes in Sleep Patterns:** Trouble sleeping, nightmares, or excessive sleeping could be signs of emotional distress caused by online bullying.

Emotional and Psychological Indicators:

- **Unexplained Mood Swings:** Sudden sadness, irritability, or anger without an apparent reason.
- **Low Self-Esteem:** Your child may start making negative comments about themselves.
- **Loss of Interest in School or Hobbies:** If they used to enjoy certain activities but now avoid them, cyberbullying could be a factor.
- **Self-Harm or Talk of Suicide:** Any mention of self-harm or suicidal thoughts must be taken seriously and addressed immediately with professional help.

If you notice any of these signs, take the situation seriously. Your child may not readily admit to being cyberbullied, so approaching the topic with care and reassurance is essential.

Steps to Take if Your Child is a Victim

Discovering that your child is being cyberbullied can be distressing, but taking immediate and supportive action can help them feel safe and empowered.

Step 1: Stay Calm and Listen

- Reassure your child that they are not alone and that you are there to help.
- Avoid overreacting or blaming them for the situation.
- Let them share their experiences without interruption, offering comfort and understanding.

Step 2: Gather Evidence

- Ask your child to save screenshots, messages, emails, or any other form of cyberbullying.
- Note the time, date, and platform where the harassment occurred.
- If possible, document usernames or any identifying details of the bully.

Step 3: Strengthen Privacy Settings

- Review and adjust privacy settings on social media, games, and messaging apps.
- Teach your child how to block and report users who send harmful messages.
- Encourage them to limit who can contact them online.

Step 4: Avoid Direct Retaliation

- Encourage your child **not** to respond to the bully, as this can escalate the situation.
- Instead, focus on documenting the harassment and taking appropriate actions.

Step 5: Provide Emotional Support

- Remind your child that bullying says more about the bully than the victim.
- Engage them in confidence-boosting activities and encourage healthy offline interactions.
- Seek professional counseling if they show signs of depression or anxiety.

Teaching Kids to Respond to Online Harassment

While adults play a crucial role in handling cyberbullying, children must also learn how to protect themselves. Teaching them the right way to respond can help prevent escalation.

1. Ignore and Block the Bully

- Tell your child that ignoring cyberbullies is often the best first step.
- Show them how to block or mute users on different platforms.

2. Do Not Engage or Retaliate

- Teach your child that responding with anger or insults only fuels the bully's behavior.
- Instead, they should disengage and report the issue to a trusted adult.

3. Keep Their Personal Information Private

- Encourage them **never** to share sensitive information such as their address, school name, or phone number online.
- Explain the dangers of sharing personal details with strangers.

4. Use the "Stop, Block, and Tell" Method

- **Stop** interacting with the bully.
- **Block** or mute the person causing harm.
- **Tell** a parent, teacher, or guardian about the situation.

When to Report Cyberbullying (to Schools, Platforms, Law Enforcement)

Not all cyberbullying incidents require external intervention, but some cases do escalate to a level where reporting becomes necessary.

1. Reporting to Social Media Platforms

Most platforms have reporting mechanisms for abusive behavior. Here's how:

- **Facebook & Instagram:** Use the built-in report option on posts and messages.
- **TikTok & Snapchat:** Report abusive users through settings.
- **YouTube:** Report inappropriate comments or videos.
- **Discord & Gaming Platforms:** Block and report toxic users.

2. Reporting to Schools

- If the cyberbullying involves classmates, school intervention may be needed.
- Provide evidence to school officials.

- Request a meeting with school counselors or administrators.
- Advocate for school policies that prevent online harassment.

3. Reporting to Law Enforcement

In severe cases, cyberbullying may become a legal issue. Report to authorities if:

- The bullying includes threats of physical harm.
- There is evidence of cyberstalking or harassment.
- Any form of sexual exploitation is involved.
- The bullying leads to extreme emotional distress or self-harm threats.

Final Thoughts

Cyberbullying is a serious issue, but with the right approach, it can be handled effectively. By educating your child on how to recognize, respond to, and report cyberbullying, you empower them to stay safe in the digital world. The key is open communication, strong online safety practices, and knowing when to seek additional help. Your child needs to know that no matter what happens online, they are never alone—and you will always be there to support them.

Chapter 11: Protecting Kids from Online Predators

The internet has opened up endless opportunities for learning, entertainment, and social interaction. However, with these benefits come significant risks, especially for children who may not fully understand the dangers that exist online. Among the most serious threats are online predators—adults who use the internet to exploit and manipulate children for personal gain. As a parent, caregiver, or educator, understanding how predators operate, recognizing warning signs, and taking immediate action can help protect children from harm.

How Predators Lure Kids Online

Online predators are skilled at manipulating children and gaining their trust. They use various techniques to appear friendly, understanding, and supportive, often posing as someone close to the child's age. Their goal is to build a relationship that makes the child feel comfortable enough to share personal information or engage in unsafe activities. Here are the most common ways predators lure kids online:

1. Fake Identities and Profiles

Predators often create fake social media or gaming accounts, pretending to be kids or teens. They may use stolen pictures, mimic teenage language, and fabricate personal stories to make their identity seem real.

2. Grooming Process

Grooming is a slow and strategic process where the predator builds trust with the child before attempting to exploit them. This process can take weeks or even months and typically follows these stages:

- **Building Trust:** The predator engages in friendly conversations, showing interest in the child's hobbies, problems, and daily life.
- **Gradual Desensitization:** They introduce inappropriate topics subtly, making the child feel comfortable discussing personal issues.
- **Isolation:** Encouraging secrecy by telling the child not to share their conversations with parents or friends.
- **Exploitation:** Eventually, the predator pressures the child into sharing personal photos, videos, or meeting in person.

3. Engaging Through Popular Platforms

Predators seek out children on platforms they frequently use, such as:

- **Social Media:** Instagram, Snapchat, TikTok, and Facebook
- **Gaming Apps:** Roblox, Fortnite, Minecraft, and Discord
- **Messaging Apps:** WhatsApp, Kik, and anonymous chat sites

4. Flattery and Emotional Manipulation

They often give excessive compliments, make the child feel special, or provide emotional support that the child may be lacking elsewhere. They might say things like, *"You're the only one who understands me"* or *"I wish I had a friend like you when I was younger."*

5. Offering Gifts or Incentives

Predators may offer in-game rewards, gift cards, or other incentives in exchange for personal information, photos, or secret communication.

6. Threats and Blackmail (Sextortion)

Once a predator has obtained sensitive images or information, they may threaten to expose the child unless they comply with further demands. This can cause extreme fear, making the child feel trapped and powerless.

Warning Signs to Watch for in Your Child's Online Behavior

Children who are being targeted by online predators often show subtle but noticeable changes in their behavior. As a parent, you should watch for the following warning signs:

1. Increased Secrecy About Online Activities

- Quickly closing tabs or hiding their screen when someone enters the room.
- Avoiding discussions about who they are talking to online.

2. Sudden Changes in Mood or Behavior

- Increased anxiety, depression, or withdrawal from family and friends.
- Becoming unusually secretive, especially about online interactions.

3. Receiving Gifts or Money from Unknown Sources

- Receiving game credits, gift cards, or physical packages without a clear explanation.
- Being reluctant to explain how they obtained them.

4. Excessive Use of Social Media or Messaging Apps

- Spending long hours chatting, especially late at night.
- Refusing to let parents check their devices or messages.

5. Using a Second or Hidden Online Account

- Creating secret social media or email accounts parents are unaware of.
- Deleting messages or browser history frequently.

6. Sudden Change in Online Friends List

- Having many new online friends, particularly older individuals.
- Becoming obsessed with chatting with one specific person.

7. Expressing a Desire to Meet Someone They Met Online

- Making secret plans to go out without explaining where they are going.

- Becoming defensive when asked about their online interactions.

Steps to Take If You Suspect Online Grooming

If you suspect that a predator is trying to groom your child, it is important to act immediately. Here's what you should do:

1. Stay Calm and Supportive

- Avoid immediately blaming or punishing your child, as this may push them to hide information.
- Create a safe space where they feel comfortable talking about their experiences.

2. Talk to Your Child Openly

- Ask open-ended questions like, *"Have you met any new friends online?"* or *"Has anyone ever made you feel uncomfortable online?"*
- Assure them that they are not in trouble and that they can always come to you for help.

3. Check Their Devices and Accounts

- Review their messages, chat history, and social media activity.
- Look for any concerning conversations, threats, or inappropriate content.

4. Change Account Settings and Passwords

- Block and report the predator's account.

- Enable stricter privacy settings on all platforms.
- Consider setting up parental controls or monitoring software.

5. Seek Professional Help If Needed

- If your child is emotionally distressed, consider talking to a counselor or therapist.
- Encourage open communication about online safety moving forward.

Reporting Suspicious Activity

If you suspect that a predator is targeting your child, reporting the incident is crucial to prevent further harm and protect other children. Here's how you can report online threats:

1. Report on the Platform

Most social media and gaming platforms have built-in reporting tools. Look for options to report inappropriate behavior, harassment, or suspicious accounts.

2. Contact Local Law Enforcement

If you believe your child is in immediate danger, call your local police or cybercrime unit.

3. Report to National Cybercrime Agencies

Different countries have agencies dedicated to handling online exploitation cases. Some examples include:

- **U.S.:** National Center for Missing & Exploited Children (NCMEC) via CyberTipline.

- **UK:** Child Exploitation and Online Protection (CEOP).
- **Canada:** Cybertip.ca.

4. Inform Your Child's School

If your child is being targeted by someone connected to their school community, informing school authorities may help prevent further contact.

5. Educate and Empower Your Child

Once you have taken action, continue to educate your child about the dangers of online predators. Reinforce the importance of:

- Never sharing personal information online.
- Avoiding private conversations with strangers.
- Immediately telling a trusted adult if they feel uncomfortable.

Final Thoughts

Protecting children from online predators requires vigilance, education, and open communication. By staying informed, setting clear boundaries, and fostering a trusting relationship with your child, you can empower them to navigate the digital world safely. Remember, the best defense against online threats is awareness and proactive action. Stay engaged, stay informed, and most importantly, stay connected with your child's online experiences.

Part 5: Advanced Strategies for Digital Parenting

Chapter 12: Raising Tech-Savvy and Responsible Digital Citizens

In today's world, raising children who are not only comfortable with technology but also responsible digital citizens is crucial. The internet offers incredible opportunities for learning, communication, and creativity, but it also comes with risks and ethical challenges. Parents and educators must teach children how to engage with digital platforms responsibly, think critically about the information they encounter, and use technology in ways that benefit both themselves and others.

This chapter will guide you through essential strategies for helping your child become a tech-savvy and ethical digital citizen. We will cover how to teach kids ethical online behavior, help them navigate misinformation and fake news, and encourage responsible technology use in schools.

Teaching Kids Ethical Online Behavior

The internet is a vast space where interactions happen quickly, often without face-to-face accountability. Teaching children ethical online behavior means helping them understand that their actions in digital spaces have real-world consequences. Just like in real life, kindness, honesty, and respect should guide their online interactions.

Understanding Digital Ethics

Digital ethics refers to the moral principles that guide behavior in online spaces. These principles include:

- **Respecting others** – Treating people online as they would in person.
- **Protecting privacy** – Understanding what information should and should not be shared.
- **Avoiding harmful behavior** – Refraining from cyberbullying, spreading rumors, or engaging in harmful online activities.
- **Being honest** – Avoiding plagiarism, misinformation, and fake identities.

Children need to understand that what they post, share, or comment on the internet can have lasting effects. Even deleted posts can be archived or screenshotted, meaning nothing is ever truly erased online.

Steps to Teach Ethical Online Behavior

- **Discuss the Golden Rule of the Internet**. Teach kids to ask themselves, "Would I say this to someone's face?" before posting anything online.
- **Explain Digital Footprints**. Show them how every action online—comments, likes, shares—leaves a digital trail that can impact their future.
- **Set Online Communication Guidelines**. Encourage positive interactions and discourage hate speech or negative comments.
- **Teach the Importance of Permission**. Remind kids that they should always ask before sharing photos or personal details of others online.
- **Encourage Reporting and Blocking Harmful Content**. Let them know they should report cyberbullying or inappropriate content rather than engaging in it.

By consistently reinforcing these principles, children will develop a strong sense of responsibility in their online interactions.

Helping Kids Navigate Misinformation and Fake News

The internet is filled with an overwhelming amount of information, not all of which is true. Misinformation and fake news can spread quickly, influencing young minds and shaping their understanding of the world. It is essential to equip children with the skills to critically evaluate online information.

Understanding Fake News and Misinformation

Misinformation refers to false or misleading content that is spread, often unintentionally. Fake news, on the other hand, is deliberately created to deceive or manipulate opinions. These can come in various forms:

- **Clickbait Headlines** – Sensational or exaggerated titles designed to attract clicks.
- **Deepfake Videos and Edited Images** – Manipulated media that presents false events as real.
- **Biased News Reports** – Articles that present only one side of an issue without evidence.
- **Unverified Social Media Claims** – Posts shared without fact-checking.

Steps to Teach Kids Critical Thinking About Online Content

Teach the 5 Ws of Evaluating Information

- **Who** created this content?
- **What** is the purpose of this content?
- **Where** was this published?
- **When** was it written?
- **Why** is it being shared?

Encourage Fact-Checking. Show kids how to use fact-checking websites like Snopes or Google's Fact Check Explorer.

Differentiate Between Opinion and Fact. Help them understand the difference between news articles, editorials, and opinion pieces.

Verify Sources Before Sharing. Encourage children to look for multiple reputable sources before believing or sharing information.

Recognize Emotional Manipulation. Teach them to be skeptical of articles that use fear, outrage, or extreme emotions to push a message.

By developing these skills, children can become responsible consumers of information and avoid spreading falsehoods online.

Encouraging Responsible Technology Use in Schools

Technology is an essential tool in education, but it must be used wisely. Schools are increasingly incorporating digital tools for learning, and children need to understand how to use these resources responsibly.

Why Responsible Tech Use Matters in Schools

- **Enhances Learning** – When used correctly, technology can support creativity and collaboration.
- **Reduces Distractions** – Excessive screen time or off-task behavior can hinder academic performance.
- **Protects Student Privacy** – Understanding digital safety ensures students do not expose sensitive information.

Strategies to Promote Responsible Technology Use in Schools

Set Clear Digital Rules in the Classroom

- Teachers and parents should discuss rules about using technology during school hours.
- Examples: "Use devices only for educational purposes" and "No texting during lessons."

Teach Digital Citizenship as Part of the Curriculum

- Schools should incorporate lessons on ethical online behavior, privacy, and cyberbullying.

Use Technology for Active Learning, Not Just Consumption

- Encourage kids to create digital projects, presentations, or videos instead of just watching content passively.

Monitor Screen Time and Encourage Breaks

- Implement tech breaks during the school day to balance screen time with physical activity.

Promote Open Discussions About Digital Challenges

- Create a safe environment where students can talk about online issues and ask questions.
- When schools and parents work together to guide children in responsible tech use, students develop the skills needed to use digital tools wisely and effectively.

Conclusion

Raising tech-savvy and responsible digital citizens requires ongoing guidance, education, and open conversations. By teaching ethical online behavior, helping kids recognize misinformation, and encouraging responsible technology use in schools, we can equip them with the skills needed to navigate the digital world safely and wisely.

Technology is a powerful tool—one that, when used responsibly, can open doors to knowledge, creativity, and meaningful connections. As parents, educators, and mentors, our role is to ensure that children not only understand how to use technology but also how to use it ethically and for positive impact.

Chapter 13: Preparing for the Future of Technology

The Rise of AI, Virtual Reality, and the Metaverse

Technology is evolving faster than ever, shaping the way we live, work, and communicate. For children growing up in this digital era, the future will be filled with new and exciting advancements, including Artificial Intelligence (AI), Virtual Reality (VR), and the Metaverse. Understanding these concepts is crucial for parents to prepare their children for the digital world ahead.

Understanding Artificial Intelligence (AI)

AI is already a part of everyday life. Whether it's virtual assistants like Siri and Alexa, recommendation algorithms on YouTube and Netflix, or AI-powered chatbots, children are interacting with artificial intelligence without even realizing it. AI can be a powerful tool for education, creativity, and problem-solving, but it also presents challenges such as data privacy, misinformation, and ethical concerns.

How AI Affects Children's Digital Lives:

- Personalized learning tools that adapt to a child's needs.

- AI-driven social media algorithms influencing content exposure.
- Voice-activated assistants answering questions and controlling smart devices.
- AI-powered chatbots used in games and apps.

While AI offers convenience and enhanced learning opportunities, it's essential to teach children critical thinking and digital literacy. They must understand that AI-generated content may not always be accurate or unbiased.

Exploring Virtual Reality (VR)

Virtual Reality (VR) is transforming the way children experience digital content. VR headsets allow users to immerse themselves in 3D environments, whether for gaming, education, or social interaction. Schools are beginning to use VR to take students on virtual field trips, simulate real-world experiences, and enhance learning in ways that traditional methods cannot.

Potential Benefits of VR for Kids:

- Enhances interactive learning through immersive experiences.
- Encourages creativity with virtual design and world-building applications.
- Provides engaging simulations for science, history, and geography.

However, there are risks associated with VR, including eye strain, motion sickness, and prolonged screen exposure. Parents should ensure children take breaks and use VR in moderation.

Understanding the Metaverse

The Metaverse is an emerging concept that combines AI, VR, and augmented reality (AR) to create a digital universe where people can interact, socialize, and work. Companies like Meta (formerly Facebook) and Microsoft are investing heavily in developing metaverse platforms, and children will likely spend a significant part of their digital lives in these environments.

Key Features of the Metaverse:

- Virtual social spaces where users can meet and interact.
- Digital economies where users buy and sell virtual goods.
- Opportunities for education, work, and entertainment in a fully digital world.

As exciting as it sounds, the Metaverse comes with concerns about online safety, digital addiction, and privacy. Parents must guide children on safe interactions and responsible behavior in these virtual spaces.

How Emerging Tech Will Change Kids' Online Experience

Technology is continuously evolving, and children will experience digital spaces differently than past generations. The integration of AI, VR, and the Metaverse will bring both opportunities and risks.

The Shift from Passive to Immersive Experiences

Traditionally, children engaged with digital content through screens—watching videos, playing games, and reading online. The future will introduce fully immersive experiences where kids can step into digital environments, interact with AI characters, and participate in virtual classrooms.

What This Means for Parents:

- Increased need for monitoring children's interactions in virtual spaces.
- Encouraging a balance between digital experiences and real-world activities.
- Teaching digital etiquette and responsible behavior in immersive environments.

The Expansion of AI-Powered Education

AI will revolutionize learning by providing personalized tutoring, automated feedback, and interactive educational experiences.

How AI Will Impact Education:

- AI tutors will help students grasp complex concepts at their own pace.
- Virtual classrooms will adapt to different learning styles.
- AI-driven tools will provide real-time feedback on assignments and projects.

Parents should prepare by encouraging children to explore AI-powered learning responsibly and ensuring they verify information from multiple sources.

Greater Risks in Digital Security and Privacy

With more interactions happening in AI-driven and virtual environments, online safety will become more important than ever. Cyber threats, deepfake technology, and AI-generated misinformation will challenge children's ability to distinguish between real and fake content.

Steps Parents Can Take:

- Teach children about deepfake videos and misinformation.
- Encourage strong digital security practices, including two-factor authentication.
- Discuss the importance of protecting personal data in digital interactions.

Preparing Kids for Future Digital Trends

As technology advances, children will need the skills and knowledge to navigate the digital world safely and effectively. Parents play a crucial role in preparing them for the future.

1. Foster Critical Thinking Skills

With AI-generated content and virtual experiences becoming mainstream, children must develop the ability to analyze and question digital information.

How to Encourage Critical Thinking:

- Teach kids to verify online sources and cross-check information.

- Discuss how AI influences content recommendations and social media feeds.
- Encourage kids to ask, "Is this real?" before trusting digital content.

2. Teach Responsible Digital Citizenship

Being a responsible digital citizen means understanding how to behave ethically and safely online. Future digital spaces will require even more awareness of online interactions.

Key Lessons for Digital Citizenship:

- Respect for others in online communities, including the Metaverse.
- Awareness of data privacy and personal information sharing.
- Understanding the long-term impact of digital footprints.

3. Encourage Hands-On Experience with Emerging Tech

Instead of shielding children from new technology, parents should introduce them to AI, VR, and other advancements in a controlled, educational way.

Ways to Introduce Kids to Future Tech:

- Use kid-friendly AI tools like voice assistants and AI learning platforms.
- Explore educational VR experiences together.
- Teach kids the basics of coding and machine learning.

4. Set Boundaries for Screen Time and Immersion

The more engaging and immersive technology becomes, the harder it will be to unplug. Parents should establish clear guidelines for when and how digital tools are used.

Tips for Healthy Tech Usage:

- Set screen time limits and encourage outdoor activities.
- Use parental controls to manage VR and Metaverse interactions.
- Model healthy tech habits by balancing screen use within the family.

5. Stay Informed and Involved

Technology changes rapidly, and parents must keep up with trends to guide their children effectively.

How to Stay Updated:

- Follow tech news and updates on AI, VR, and online safety.
- Join online communities or forums for digital parenting advice.
- Engage in conversations with children about their digital experiences.

Conclusion

The future of technology will bring incredible advancements that shape the way children learn, play, and interact online. AI, VR, and the Metaverse will offer exciting opportunities, but they also come with risks that parents must prepare for. By fostering critical thinking, encouraging responsible digital citizenship, and setting healthy boundaries, parents can equip their children to navigate the digital world safely and confidently. The key is to stay informed, be involved, and embrace technology as a tool for learning and growth.

Conclusion

The Role of Parents in Shaping Digital Behavior

As we reach the conclusion of this guide, it is important to reflect on the central role that parents play in shaping their children's digital behavior. The online world is vast, complex, and constantly evolving. While it offers incredible opportunities for learning, creativity, and social connection, it also comes with risks that children may not fully understand. This is where your role as a digital parent becomes essential.

Children look to their parents for guidance, even when it may not seem obvious. The way you approach digital parenting—whether through open discussions, setting boundaries, or leading by example—will have a lasting impact on how your child interacts with technology. Your guidance helps them develop responsible habits, critical thinking skills, and the ability to navigate the internet safely.

Think of digital parenting as an ongoing journey rather than a one-time conversation. As technology advances and your child grows, their digital needs and challenges will change. The key to success is to remain actively involved, stay informed about new trends, and adapt your approach accordingly.

Leading by Example

One of the most effective ways to shape your child's digital behavior is by modeling responsible internet use. Children are observant and tend to mimic the habits of their parents. If they see you balancing screen time, prioritizing offline interactions, and practicing safe online behaviors, they are more likely to do the same. Here are a few ways to set a good example:

- Avoid excessive screen time, especially during family meals and conversations.
- Be mindful of the content you engage with online.
- Demonstrate respectful and responsible communication on social media.
- Show them how to fact-check information before believing or sharing it.

Staying Actively Involved

Being actively involved in your child's digital life does not mean spying on them or controlling every aspect of their online activity. Instead, it means being present, aware, and available to guide them when needed. Here's how you can stay involved:

- Ask about their favorite apps, websites, and games.
- Encourage them to share their online experiences, both positive and negative.
- Regularly review and adjust privacy settings together.
- Be approachable so they feel comfortable discussing concerns with you.

By staying engaged, you create a sense of trust that allows your child to turn to you when they encounter challenges or dangers online.

Final Digital Parenting Checklist

To help reinforce all the key principles discussed in this book, here is a final checklist to ensure your child has a safe and healthy digital experience. This checklist serves as a practical guide that you can revisit and update as needed:

1. Online Safety Basics

- Set up strong passwords and enable two-factor authentication for accounts.
- Teach your child to recognize phishing scams and suspicious links.
- Enable Safe Search on Google and Restricted Mode on YouTube.
- Discuss the risks of oversharing personal information.

2. Social Media and Communication

- Review and adjust privacy settings on all social media accounts.
- Explain the importance of only accepting friend requests from people they know.
- Teach them how to block and report inappropriate behavior.
- Encourage them to think before posting or commenting online.

3. Screen Time and Healthy Digital Habits

- Establish and enforce screen time limits based on age and needs.
- Promote a balanced routine that includes offline activities.
- Set device-free times, such as during meals and before bedtime.
- Educate them on the importance of eye health and posture when using devices.

4. Cyberbullying and Online Threats

- Teach your child how to identify and respond to cyberbullying.
- Encourage them to speak up if they or a friend are being harassed online.
- Discuss the dangers of online predators and how they can manipulate children.
- Remind them to never meet online acquaintances in person without parental supervision.

5. Digital Footprint and Critical Thinking

- Explain that everything posted online can be permanent.
- Teach them to fact-check information before sharing.
- Discuss the importance of ethical and respectful online behavior.
- Show them how to verify the credibility of news and online sources.

This checklist is not a one-time tool but something you can revisit and update regularly. Digital trends will change, and so will your child's online activities. Keeping this checklist handy will ensure that you maintain a proactive and informed approach to digital parenting.

Encouraging Open Communication About Online Safety

Perhaps the most important takeaway from this guide is that open communication is the foundation of effective digital parenting. When children feel they can openly discuss their online experiences without fear of punishment or judgment, they are more likely to seek guidance and report issues when they arise.

Building Trust Through Honest Conversations

Start by making online safety discussions a natural part of everyday conversations. Rather than lecturing, ask open-ended questions that encourage dialogue. For example:

- "What's the most interesting thing you've seen online lately?"
- "Have you ever come across something online that made you uncomfortable?"
- "How do you decide which friend requests or messages to accept?"

By asking these types of questions, you show that you are interested in their online world and that they can talk to you without fear.

Creating a Safe Space for Sharing

Children need to feel that they can talk to you about their digital experiences without immediate punishment. If they make a mistake or encounter something harmful, your first response should be supportive rather than punitive. Some ways to create a safe space include:

- React calmly when they share concerns or admit to mistakes.
- Reassure them that everyone makes errors and that learning from them is important.
- Help them find solutions instead of simply banning apps or devices.

Keeping Communication Ongoing

Online safety is not a one-time discussion—it should be an ongoing conversation. Set regular check-ins where you casually talk about their digital activities. These check-ins don't have to be formal; they can happen while driving, during meals, or before bedtime. Regular conversations ensure that your child feels comfortable bringing up concerns whenever needed.

Final Thoughts

Digital parenting is a dynamic and evolving responsibility. While the internet presents risks, it also provides incredible opportunities for education, creativity, and connection. Your role is to equip your child with the knowledge, skills, and confidence to navigate the digital world safely and responsibly.

Remember, you don't have to be a tech expert to be an effective digital parent. What matters most is staying engaged, fostering open communication, and leading by example. By taking a proactive and supportive approach, you are setting your child up for a safe and positive online experience.

Thank you for taking the time to invest in your child's digital safety. Your efforts today will shape their ability to use technology responsibly for years to come.

Additional Resources

As a parent, having access to the right tools and resources can make all the difference in ensuring your child's online safety. In this section, we provide two valuable resources:

- **A Parental Control Apps Comparison Chart** – A detailed breakdown of popular parental control apps, helping you decide which one is best for your family.
- **A List of Safe Websites & Apps for Kids** – A carefully curated list of platforms that are fun, educational, and child-friendly, so you can confidently guide your kids to safe online experiences.

Each resource is designed to support you in navigating the digital landscape with confidence and making informed decisions about your child's online activities.

Parental Control Apps Comparison Chart

Why Parental Control Apps Are Essential

Parental control apps are one of the most effective tools for supervising your child's online activity without needing to be constantly present. They provide parents with the ability to:

- **Monitor Screen Time:** Track how much time your child spends on devices and set limits.
- **Filter Content:** Block inappropriate websites, apps, or content.
- **Track Location:** Some apps allow GPS tracking for added safety.
- **Monitor Social Media & Messages:** Some advanced apps help detect cyberbullying, online predators, or other harmful interactions.

However, not all parental control apps are the same. Some offer advanced features, while others focus on simplicity. The chart below provides a side-by-side comparison of some of the most widely used parental control apps, highlighting their key features and usability.

Parental Control Apps Comparison Chart

App Name	Screen Time Limits	Content Filtering	Location Tracking	Social Media Monitoring	Best For
Qustodio	✅ Yes	✅ Yes	✅ Yes	✅ Yes	Comprehensive monitoring
Bark	✅ Yes	✅ Yes	❌ No	✅ Yes	Social media monitoring
Net Nanny	✅ Yes	✅ Yes	✅ Yes	❌ No	Content filtering
Google Family Link	✅ Yes	✅ Yes	✅ Yes	❌ No	Free basic control
Norton Family	✅ Yes	✅ Yes	✅ Yes	✅ Yes	Best for multiple devices

Each app has its strengths, and the right choice depends on your family's needs.

Choosing the Right Parental Control App

When selecting an app, consider the following:

- **Age of Your Child:** Younger kids may only need basic filtering, while teenagers may require social media monitoring.
- **Device Compatibility:** Ensure the app works on all your child's devices.
- **Ease of Use:** Some apps are more user-friendly than others.
- **Budget:** Free options exist, but premium apps offer more advanced features.

By using a parental control app, you create a safer digital environment for your child while maintaining their sense of privacy and independence.

List of Safe Websites & Apps for Kids

Why It's Important to Guide Kids Toward Safe Online Spaces

The internet is filled with both positive and negative content. While harmful websites and unsafe apps pose risks, many kid-friendly platforms provide educational, creative, and entertaining experiences in a secure environment.

To ensure that children have safe and enriching online experiences, parents should introduce them to websites and apps that are designed specifically for kids. These platforms often include built-in parental controls, child-friendly content, and minimal exposure to ads or inappropriate materials.

Below is a curated list of websites and apps that offer a safe and fun online experience for children of various ages.

Safe Websites & Apps for Kids

Category	Recommended Websites & Apps
Educational Websites	- **PBS Kids** – Interactive learning games and videos - **National Geographic Kids** – Fun facts, games, and videos about nature and animals - **Khan Academy Kids** – Free educational lessons for young children
Creative & Art Apps	- **Toca Life World** – A creative sandbox game for kids - **Crayola Create & Play** – Drawing and coloring activities - **Lego Life** – A safe community for kids to share LEGO creations
Safe Social Apps	- **Messenger Kids** – A safe way for kids to chat with approved friends and family - **Kinzoo** – A private and secure social app for kids
Reading & Storytelling Apps	- **Epic!** – A vast library of digital books for kids - **Storyline Online** – Videos of books read by celebrities - **Libby** – Free digital books through local libraries
Safe Gaming Apps	- **Animal Jam** – A safe online multiplayer game about animals - **Minecraft (Education Edition)** – A creative and educational version of Minecraft - **Prodigy Math Game** – A fun way to practice math skills
STEM & Coding Apps	- **ScratchJr** – A beginner-friendly coding platform - **Tynker** – Coding games and lessons for kids - **Lightbot** – A puzzle game that teaches programming logic

Encouraging Safe Online Exploration

Introducing your child to safe websites and apps not only protects them but also encourages them to develop positive digital habits. Here are a few tips to make their online experience both fun and secure:

- **Use Kid-Safe Browsers:** Install child-friendly search engines like **Kiddle** or **KidRex** to prevent exposure to harmful content.
- **Supervise Younger Kids:** Sit with your child when they explore new websites or apps.

- **Set Content Restrictions:** Many apps and websites allow parental control settings to block inappropriate content.

By guiding your child toward safe digital spaces, you foster a positive relationship with technology while minimizing online risks.

Final Thoughts

The **Parental Control Apps Comparison Chart** and **List of Safe Websites & Apps for Kids** are designed to be practical resources you can refer to whenever needed. Protecting your child in the digital world is a continuous process, but with the right tools, you can ensure they have a safe and enjoyable online experience.